EAU CLAIRE DISTRICT LIBRARY
6528 East Main Street
P.O. Box 328
EAU CLAIRE, MI 49111

J
512.7
Mid

W9-BAI-182

World Book, Inc.
233 N. Michigan Avenue
Chicago, IL 60601
U.S.A.

For information about other World Book publications,
visit our website at www.worldbook.com
or call 1-800-WORLDBK (967-5325).
For information about sales to schools and libraries,
call 1-800-975-3250 (United States),
or 1-800-837-5365 (Canada).

©2013 World Book, Inc. All rights reserved. This volume
may not be reproduced in whole or in part in any form
without prior written permission from the publisher.

WORLD BOOK and the GLOBE DEVICE are registered
trademarks or trademarks of World Book, Inc.

Library of Congress Cataloging-in-Publication Data

Numbers.
       pages cm. -- (Building blocks of mathematics)
    Summary: "A graphic nonfiction volume that introduces
the history of numbers and number systems"-- Provided
by publisher.
    Includes index.
    ISBN 978-0-7166-1436-4 -- ISBN 978-0-7166-1477-7 (pbk.)
    1.  Number concept--Comic books, strips, etc.--Juvenile
literature. 2.  Numbers, Natural--Comic books, strips,
etc.--Juvenile literature. 3.  Graphic novels.  I. World
Book, Inc.
    QA141.15.N845 2013
    512.7--dc23
                              2012031038

Building Blocks of Mathematics
ISBN: 978-0-7166-1431-9 (set, hc.)

Printed in China by Shenzhen Donnelley
Printing Co., Ltd., Guangdong Province
2nd printing October 2013

Acknowledgments:
Created by Samuel Hiti and Joseph Midthun
Art by Samuel Hiti
Written by Joseph Midthun
Special thanks to Anita Wager, Hala
Ghousseini, and Syril McNally.

STAFF
Executive Committee
President: Donald D. Keller
Vice President and Editor in Chief:
    Paul A. Kobasa
Vice President, Sales & Marketing:
    Sean Lockwood
Vice President, International: Richard Flower
Director, Human Resources: Bev Ecker

Editorial
Manager, Series and Trade: Cassie Mayer
Writer and Letterer: Joseph Midthun
Researcher: Lynn Durbin
Manager, Contracts & Compliance
    (Rights & Permissions): Loranne K. Shields

Manufacturing/Pre-Press
Director: Carma Fazio
Manufacturing Manager: Steven Hueppchen
Production/Technology Manager:
    Anne Fritzinger
Proofreader: Emilie Schrage

Graphics and Design
Senior Manager, Graphics and Design: Tom Evans
Coordinator, Design Development and
    Production: Brenda B. Tropinski
Book Design: Samuel Hiti

# TABLE OF CONTENTS

There is a glossary on page 30. Terms defined in the glossary are in type **that looks like this** on their first appearance.

We're the **base ten** system— 10 numbers that make up all other numbers!

You can use us to make any number you can think of!

Yeah, but where do we come from?

Good question!

Humans invented numbers a long time ago.

Raawwrrg!

Nope, I'm pretty sure it was humans.

We don't know *exactly* where or when numbers were invented, but we have some good clues...

# EARLY COUNTING METHODS

We *do* know that people didn't always use written numbers.

They likely counted on their fingers when they were out and about.

To keep track of an amount, people etched tally marks on cave walls.

Or a piece of wood!

Or stones!

Or bones!

Each tally mark stood for *one* thing.

Much later, people invented names for different numbers.

Then they started to arrange the names in order by size.

That's counting!

At some point, ancient Egyptians started to use different objects to represent groups of 10 things.

For instance, a single stone might stand for a herd of 10 sheep.

This idea made counting large numbers of things faster and easier!

Today, we continue to represent large numbers by using groups of 10.

That's why we call ourselves the base ten **number system!**

# NUMBER WORDS

The numbers 1 through 10 have special names in most languages because people learned to count by using their bodies.

You can count up to 10 on your fingers and then start over.

Let's try!

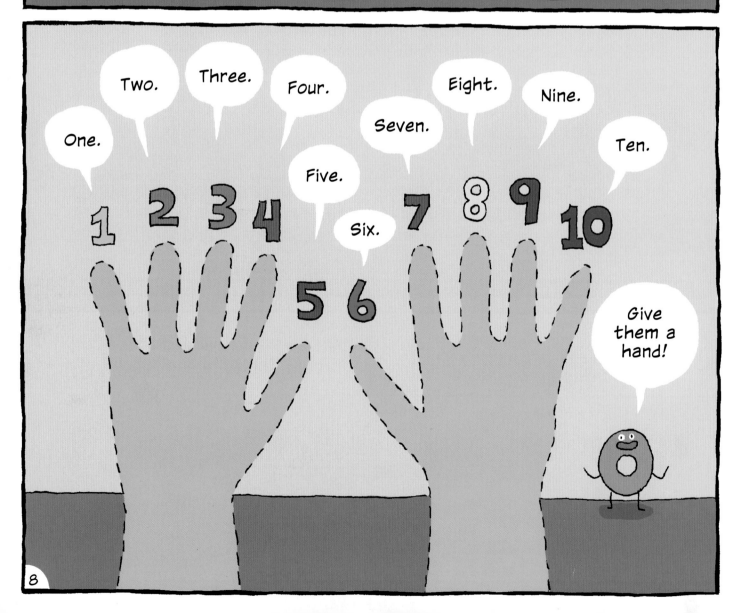

The ancient Egyptians used a system based on groups of 10.

Eventually, people developed number systems, or ways of counting and naming numbers.

Like you, they used symbols called numerals. Each numeral represented a certain amount.

The Egyptians had special symbols for their numbers, like these:

1    10    100

They also had symbols for big numbers like 1,000.

For 1,000, the Egyptians drew a picture of the lotus flower.

TINK TINK    TINK TINK

There are thousands of lotus flowers in the Nile River, even now!

EAU CLAIRE DISTRICT LIBRARY

But the Greeks used the letters of their alphabet to write numbers.

Like the Egyptians, the ancient Greeks counted by groups of 10.

The first nine letters stood for ones, from 1 through 9.

The ancient Chinese also counted by groups of 10.

They performed calculations using rods made of animal bones or bamboo.

Early Chinese numerals looked like these rods:

But base ten isn't the only way people counted.

After a while, the Romans found a way to save time and space when writing out their numbers.

We used subtraction to make new symbols for the numbers 4 and 9.

The numeral *IIII* became *IV* and the numeral *VIIII* became *IX*...

*These new symbols follow a rule:*

The smaller numeral goes before the larger numeral to show that it is being subtracted.

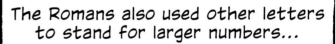

The Romans also used other letters to stand for larger numbers...

L = 50
C = 100
D = 500

# SHOWING NOTHING

Wait—I almost forgot to introduce you to one of the most important concepts of mathematics—

Me!

I'm Zero!

You use me to show *no amount*. Zip, zed, nada!

Some number systems had ways to work around using a value for nothing.

The Romans and Egyptians had symbols for 10, 100, and more. But they had nothing for me...

Showing *nothing* as a *symbol* proved difficult—

But *I can do it!*

For example, to show the number 30, you can separate 3 beads in the tens column...

...and *none* in the ones column.

CLICK

# GLOSSARY

**abacus** a frame with rows of counters or beads used for adding and other tasks in arithmetic. The abacus was used by the ancient Greeks and Romans and in China and other Asian countries. Today, it is used in schools.

**Babylonian** having to do with Babylonia, an ancient region in what is now southern Iraq. Babylonia was the site of several kingdoms.

**base ten** a number system that uses 10 basic symbols: 1, 2, 3, 4, 5, 6, 7, 8, 9, and 0. The value of any of these symbols depends on the place it occupies in the number.

**binary number** a number written with only two digits: 1 and 0.

**Hindu** one of a group of people living in India.

**number system** a way of writing numbers. People in most parts of the world use the base ten number system.

**place value** the value of a digit as determined by its place in a number.

**Mesopotamia** an ancient region in the Middle East where the world's earliest cities were built.

**Roman** a citizen of ancient Rome.

# FIND OUT MORE

## BOOKS

**Fun with Roman Numerals**
by David A. Adler and Edward Miller
(Holiday House, 2008)

**How Many Donkeys?**
An Arabic Counting Tale
by Margaret Read MacDonald,
Nadia Jameel Taibah,
and Carol Liddiment
(Albert Whitman, 2009)

**Leaping Lizards**
by Stuart J. Murphy
and JoAnn Adinolfi
(HarperCollins, 2005)

**More or Less: A Rain Forest**
Counting Book
by Rebecca Fjelland Davis
(Capstone Press, 2007)

**On Beyond a Million:**
An Amazing Math Journey
by David M. Schwartz
and Paul Meisel
(Random House, 1999)

**One Is a Snail, Ten Is a Crab:**
A Counting by Feet Book
by April Pulley Sayre,
Jeff Sayre, and Randy Cecil
(Candlewick Press, 2003)

**The Story of Our Numbers:**
The History of Arabic Numbers
by Zelda King
(PowerKids Press, 2004)

**Teeth, Tails and Tentacles:**
An Animal Counting Book
by Christopher Wormell
(Running Press Kids, 2004)

## WEBSITES

**1, 2, 3 Counting Games**
pbskids.org/games/counting.html
Join your favorite PBS characters
in learning about numbers
and counting.

**ABCya!**
www.abcya.com
Choose your grade level to find
number and counting games that
are just right for you!

**Count Us In**
abc.net.au/countusin
The games and activities at this
site are perfect for practicing
number skills.

**Gamequarium: Place Value Games**
www.gamequarium.com/placevalue.html
This teacher-designed website
provides many pages of games
for practice with place value
and other number skills.

**Roman Numerals Games**
www.roman-numerals.org/games.html
Learn about Roman numerals here
and test your knowledge as you go!

**Tamba's Abacus**
www.bbc.co.uk/cbeebies/tikkabilla/
games/tikkabilla - tambasabacus
Sing and count along with a
colorful online abacus at this
site from the BBC.

# INDEX

abacus, 18-21, 26-27
alphabet, 14, 16-17
Arabic numerals.
  See Hindu-Arabic numerals
Arabs, ancient, 22, 27

Babylonians, 15
base ten system, 5
  beginning of, 7
  in Arabic numerals, 24-25
  number names in, 8-11
  of Chinese, 14
  of Egyptians, 7, 12-13
  of Greeks, 14
  on abacus, 19
binary number system, 28-29

Chinese, ancient, 14
counting
  early methods of, 6-7, 12-13
  on abacus, 18-21
  on fingers, 8-9
  See also numbers

Egyptians, ancient, 7, 12-13, 26

Greeks, ancient, 14

Hindu-Arabic numerals, 22-23, 28
  place value in, 24-25
  zero in, 27

India, 22

lotus symbol, 12-13

Maya, 15, 27

numbers, 4-5
  Babylonian, 15
  Chinese, 14
  Egyptian, 6-7, 12-13
  Greek, 14
  Hindu-Arabic, 22-23
  invention of, 5
  Mayan, 15
  Roman, 16-17
  words for, 8-11

See also base ten system; counting

place value, 23-25

Roman numerals, 16-17, 25
  addition with, 23
  zero in, 26
Romans, 16-17
  abacus of, 18

sifr, 27
sunya, 27

tally marks, 6

zero
  and place value, 24-25
  invention of, 26-27

EAU CLAIRE DISTRICT LIBRARY